Little

Book of

Wales

Zymurgy Publishing, 2005

A CIP catalogue record for this book is available from the British library.
Cover design Nick Ridley
Printed & bound in Great Britain by
William Clowes Ltd, Beccles, Suffolk

ISBN 1 903506 17 4

Published by Zymurgy Publishing,
Newcastle upon Tyne
1098765432

For Aejiz (1976-2005)

You were the most exquisite protector and guide whose footprints were light but leave a rich and considerable legacy.

Thanks to Simon - for the music and candid counsel.

"Wales is a singular noun but a plural experience."

(Professor Dai Smith)

Forewarner

The *Little Book of Wales* is a capsule book for those too pushed for time or energy to read *A Welsh Miscellany* (by the same author and publisher). It is a *skinny cappuccino* of a read with extra froth and a vehement WELCOME at the till side.

Population

2,903,085

Sheep to Peep Ratio

4:1 (there are over 11 million sheep)

Geographical Spread

22% of the population [people not sheep - let's not be flippant] were born in Wales but live in England.

"*You need half a pint of phlegm in your throat just to pronounce the place-names.*"

(Quoted from Blackadder III)

The Celtic languages have 6th century roots. They were affected by Latin which led to the development of Welsh, Cornish and Breton. The Welsh themselves are in fact an Anglo-Saxon invention - from 'weala(s)' meaning 'foreigner(s)'.

Language Renaissance

Today, Welsh is the most widely spoken of the Celtic languages (600,000+ in Wales alone - Census 2001). It has come so far in fact that Microsoft has launched Welsh Windows™, recognising its "linguistic diversity".

Welsh Described

Welsh is a phonemic and largely phonetic language so what you see is what you get. This, told as seen, facet of the language gives those unfamiliar with it the ability to pronounce the written word relatively easily [except, perhaps, the lateral voiceless alveolar fricatives - the Ll or ll sound].

Alphabet

A B C CH D Dd E F Ff G Ng H
I L Ll M N O P Ph R Rh S T Th U
W Y

a b c ch d dd e f ff g ng h i l ll m n
o p ph r rh s t th u w y

The Vowels

A E I O U W Y + sometimes H

a e i o u w y + sometimes h

J-Low

The letter 'J' is absent in the Welsh alphabet. James and Jones are very popular surnames in Wales and likely explanations for this quirk is that John and Ieuan have become corrupted and that *Siâm*(s) and *Siôn* have been anglicised over the years.

In the Name of the Father

Welsh surnames are generally patronymic i.e. derived from the father's name and a relic of *ap* ('son of'). Therefore many surnames either begin 'b' or 'p':

ap Owen   = Bowen
ap Hugh/Huw = Pugh/Puw
ap Howell   = Powell
ap Robert   = Probert

Welsh Derivatives

Welsh is one of the oldest European languages, some English words have a Welsh provenance. For example:

Coracle - a small rounded boat

Cromlech - arched stone

Cwm - valley

Eisteddfod - session/sitting

Flummery - a pudding, flattery

Gorsedd - throne

Hwyl - enjoyment, sail

Expressions

Cnychu - Fuck*

Cnycha/Cnychu Bant - Fuck Off*

Cymru am Byth - Wales Forever

Diawl/Y Diawl - Devil/The Devil

Iechyd Da - Literally 'good health'

Uffern - Hell

Uffern Dân - Hell Fire

Ych a Fi/Ach a Fi - Yuck

*Extreme caution recommended due to the emotional fervour attached

Communication Breakdown

Prior to devolution the Welsh Office installed a sign near Cardiff announcing impending roadworks. It read "Cynllwyn gan y Swyddfa Gymreig...". Rather than being a "Plan by the Welsh Office..." to improve the road, the sign foretold of a "conspiracy". *Cynllyn* is Welsh for plan and not "*cynllwyn*" as appeared.

Sealyham Terrier

A short-legged, wire-haired, breed of terrier with a medium length white coat. Often shortened to Sealyham as it takes its name from the village in south-west Wales that first bred it in the 19th century.

Welsh

Of or relating to Wales or its people, language or culture.

Or

A white long-bodied, lop-eared, breed of pig primarily kept for bacon.

Welsh Black

A native cattle breed and one of the UK's oldest, is the hardy Welsh Black. The breed dates back to the Celtic pre-Roman period and can be found overseas including the USA, Canada, Australia, New Zealand and Germany.

Welsh Cob

A breed of pony and cob renowned for their versatility, superior performance, hardiness and kind nature.

Their breeding is divided into four 'Sections': Section A (Welsh Mountain Pony), Section B (Welsh Pony), Section C (Welsh Pony [Cob Type]) and Section D (Welsh Cob).

Welsh Corgi

The full name for corgi - a short-legged breed of dog with a fox like head, originally from Wales. Comes from the Welsh *cor* = dwarf + *ci* = dog, i.e short/dwarf dog.

Welsh Dresser

A type of dresser. A Welsh dresser comprises a sideboard with drawers, open display shelves and storage cupboards below.

Welsh Flannel

A fine kind of flannel made from the fleece of Welsh mountain sheep, and largely manufactured by hand.

Welsh Glaive, or Welsh Hook

A weapon of war used in former times by the Welsh, commonly regarded as a kind of poleaxe.

Welsh Harp

A type of harp (a triple harp) in which the strings are arranged in three rows. Used especially for the accompaniment of singing, dancing and poetry.

Welshman's Button

A species of caddis fly. The larvae are freshwater insects which peak in summer. Used by fly fishermen as bait for trout fishing.

Welsh Mortgage

A type of mortgage, being a conveyance of an estate, redeemable at any time on payment of the principal, with an understanding that the profits in the meantime shall be received by the mortgagee without account, in satisfaction of interest.

Welsh Mountain

A common breed of small hardy sheep kept mainly in the mountains of Wales. They are territorial, learning about the mountains from their mothers.

Welsh Mountain Pony

A small, sturdy, intelligent, gentle, but graceful breed of pony, originally from Wales. Used mainly for riding, the breed has lived on mountains for over a thousand years.

Welsh Mutton

A meat obtained from the breeds of mountain sheep in Wales. Abundant grazing and the Welsh terrain contribute to the hardiness of the stock and the complexity of the meat's flavour.

Welsh Onion

A kind of onion forming clusters of bulbs, having hollow inflated stalks and leaves, but scarcely any bulb. A native of Siberia it is said to have been introduced from Germany, and is supposed to have derived its name from a German term for 'foreign'.

Welsh Parsley

Hemp, or halters made from hemp. The seeds of the hemp plant were once used in a form of folk divination.

Welsh Poppy

A perennial western European papaveraceous plant, like a poppy but with large yellow flowers, abundant in mid-Wales.

Welsh Rarebit

Originally *Welsh Rabbit* but became known as *Welsh Rarebit* by way of 18th century folk etymology. A savoury dish of melted cheese and seasoning (sometimes mixed with milk) served on toast.

Welsh Sheepdog

The Welsh sheepdog has a distinctive red colour and is recognised, as distinguishable from the border collie, as a hard-working animal with plenty of stamina. Threatened with extinction a decade ago, Welsh sheepdogs are now being exported around the world.

Welsh Terrier

A wire-haired breed of terrier with a black and tan coat.

Originally developed as a hunting dog.

Eisteddfod (Origins)

Iolo Morgannwg was born in Glamorgan (*Morgannwg* is Welsh for Glamorgan). He claimed that a unique metre was in use by the county's bards, that they would gather together in a ceremony called the *Gorsedd* (Throne) and that the tradition had continued unbroken since before the birth of Christ.

Eisteddfod (Modern)

The modern National Eisteddfod has 19th century roots and has evolved into an annual weeklong celebration of culture, tradition and language. *Eisteddfod* is a derivative of eistedd (to sit) and, in Wales particularly, culminates in the *Gorsedd* ceremonies which honour the finest prose, free verse and strict metre poetry.

St David's Day

Dewi *Sant* (St David) is patron saint of Wales and why [mainly] children get togged up on 1st March and engage in rituals of national pride - conducting mini eisteddfods/ displaying daffodils/being creative with leeks. Born in Ceredigion, he founded a monastic community where the 12th century St David's Cathedral now stands.

Eisteddfod (Modern)

The modern National Eisteddfod has 19th century roots and has evolved into an annual week long celebration of culture, tradition and language. *Eisteddfod* is a derivative of eistedd (to sit) and, in Wales particularly, culminates in the *Gorsedd* ceremonies which honour the finest prose, free verse and strict metre poetry.

Nos Galan

Nos *Galan* and *Dydd Calan* are the Welsh names for New Year's Eve and New Year's Day respectively. As the Celtic people believed that life was a continuous circle *Y Fari Lwyd* (the skull of a horse covered in white cloth and decorated with ribbons) comes back to life at this time, and is still paraded through some Welsh villages.

Love Spoons

Traditionally, it was customary to give your love a spoon carved by hand out of wood in a shape expressing a specific desire. For example, some had balls [ahem] inside the handle implying a longing for children. Love spoons are still presented today but are mostly bought from tourist shops ready-crafted.

When he was 37, a challenge came from the 'Prince' of Bedwas to run the 12 miles from Newport in Monmouthshire to Bedwas Church near Caerphilly. The race was easily won but Guto's body gave way and the 5 km Nos Galan Races, started in 1958, are held in his memory.

Calennig

Another New Year's Day custom is that of *calennig* (New Year's gift) where boys would knock on neighbours' doors carrying three legged totems, singing rhymes and splashing water. This was done to elicit a small gift from householders. Today, it is remembered by displaying oranges pierced with cloves and standing on a tripod of twigs.

National identity is robust with 67% (2001 Census) reporting their nationality as Welsh. Recent opinion polls show that the Welsh have a sense of dual identity - of being both Welsh and British.

That said, Welshness has a powerful image whether you think of dragons, daffodils, big pointy hats, sheep, rugby, Charlotte Church or the Stereophonics.

The Welsh Flag

The Welsh flag is a distinctive passant red dragon on a background of two equal horizontal green and white stripes. It is said that the mark of the dragon first appeared in Roman times, is shown on the Bayeux tapestry and was appropriated by the Tudors. *Y Ddraig Goch* (The Red Dragon) remains a symbol of national independence.

Leek

A modest vegetable used as food, the leek has became a national symbol because of its significance in the traditional Welsh diet. St David adopted it, Shakespeare wrote about it and the Tudors supplied their household guards with them for St David's Day.

Daffodil

The origins of the use of yellow daffs as a national symbol are patchy. It is most likely that the flower became associated with Wales because of its close resemblance to the word leek in Welsh. *Cenhinen/cennin* is Welsh for leek(s) and *cenhinen/ Cennin Pedr* is Welsh for daffodil(s).

St Patrick

St Patrick was Welsh. A south Wales mining village, Banwen in the Dulais Valley, claims St Patrick as a former resident. Many historians and historical accounts relate that he was captured as a teenager by Irish slavers and shipped over the water.

Patagonia

During the 19th century industrialisation and urbanisation that threatened the demise of the Welsh language 153 men, women and children embarked on a journey across the Atlantic in search of a better life. Arriving in 1865 aboard the *Mimosa* they colonised the first land they reached in southern Argentina.

Y Wladfa (colony/settlement) was established and subsequent generations moved on to Chile where the landscape is reminiscent of home. Spanish influences are natural of course and the quirk of two colliding cultures has birthed children with hybrid names like Pablo Jenkins and Juan Jones in the farmhouses and teashops flying the Welsh flag.

Namesake

America was apparently named after Welshman Richard Amerik for being principal investor in John Cabot's transatlantic expedition of 1497. A year later Amerigo Vespucci was credited with the same. Observers conclude that Amerik gave his name to North America and Vespucci to South (otherwise we would have a continent called 'Vespuccia').

Pioneers

Rowland Ellis lead fellow Quakers in the 17th century to Pennsylvania from Bryn Mawr farm in Dolgellau. A replica of the farm gave its name to a town there. Families of Welsh extraction remain in Pennsylvania and similarly there is a Bethesda in Maryland. Evidence also exists of a Cardiff in New Jersey and a suburb called 'Welsh' in Los Angeles.

Tie a Yellow Ribbon

Way before the 1973 hit 'Tie a Yellow Ribbon Round the Ole Oak Tree' Welsh settlers in America planted daffodils outside their homes to welcome new arrivals. Later on they used yellow ribbon tied around a tree instead.

Pioneers

Rowland Ellis led fellow Quakers in the 17th century to Pennsylvania from Bryn Mawr farm in Dolgellau. A replica of the farm gave its name to a town there. Families of Welsh extraction remain in Pennsylvania and similarly there is a Bethesda in Maryland. Evidence also exists of a Cardiff in New Jersey and a suburb called 'Welsh' in Los Angeles.

Bad Boy Inc

Al Capone's accountant, a Llewelyn (Murray the Hump) Humphreys, came from a Powys family, was once America's 'most wanted man' and took control of the *Mob* following the imprisonment of his employer.

Landmark Achievements

In terms of geography and architecture, Welshmen and their decendants are responsible for New York's Guggenheim Museum (Frank Lloyd Wright), Ellis Island (Samuel Ellis) and Grand Central Station (John Belle).

Land of My Fathers?

New York's Manhattan is arguably Welsh-owned. Billions of dollars are said to be owing to descendants of Robert Edwards who was allegedly given the land by the Crown. The *Edwards Millions/Manhattan Millions* has involved hundreds of Welsh families in litigation, claiming back rent from the island, since the 19th century.

Park Life

Welsh emigrant Col. Griffith J Griffith gave the City of Los Angeles the 3,015 acres of land which now comprises the core of Griffith Park and contains the Griffith Observatory.

Explorer

Sir Henry Morton Stanley from Denbigh uttered the words "Dr Livingstone I presume" when he 'found' the explorer apparently missing in Africa in search of the source of the Nile.

Down Under

The 1914 Prime Minister of Australia was Welshman William Hughes.

Rolf Harris, Danni and Kylie Minogue's ancestry can be traced back to south Wales - Merthyr Tydfil and Maesteg respectfully.

Welsh Societies

I f you think Aussies and South Africans are itinerant have a look at this. There are around 100 Welsh societies around the world (those with websites anyway) in places as diverse as:

America, Australia, Belgium, Canada, Dubai, England, Finland, France, Hong Kong, Japan, New Zealand, Norway, Russia.

"Only the soul can starve to death with food about."

(quoted from *Rape of the Fair Country* by Alexander Cordell)

The income from mining and agriculture dictated, for centuries, a very simple and basic diet in Welsh kitchens. Ingredients were largely grown, collected or caught and prepared in a pot and/or on a bakestone on an open hearth.

A modern staple, origin unknown, is now *half and half* (or *aff 'n' aff* as it is colloquially known) which is, Atkins dieters exempt, half rice and half chips.

Caerphilly Cheese

Caerphilly cheese is a crumbly, moist and creamy white vegetarian cheese traditionally of south and west Wales. The cheese first sold in the area around Caerphilly in 1830. It was produced by local farms for domestic use and miners would eat it to replace the salt lost down the pits.

Pot Noodle

The cheap student staple, although not a traditional Welsh dish, was born and brought up in Wales. The snack has been made in Wales since 1979 and currently produces 170 million pots a year from a factory at Crumlin in Gwent to cater for the rate of consumption which is said to be five a second. [Another 60 just gone then].

Captain Morgan Rum

Captain Henry Morgan was a 17th century privateer in the Caribbean. Originally from Llanrumney, he waived the rules whilst enjoying the official support of the government. Sent to break the Spanish stranglehold on the colonies he executed an attack on Portobello in 1668. The episode is commemorated in the name of the famous London street.

The Oldest Pub in Wales

The Blue Anchor in the village of East Aberthaw has traded virtually non-stop as an inn since 1380. The Listed former CAMRA *Pub of the Year* was recently reconstructed following a serious fire. Ironically, it was also Wales' *Real Fire Pub of the Year 2002*.

"What is this life if, full of care,

We have no time to stand and stare?"

(from 'Leisure' by W H Davies)

Wales has inspired writers and poets, both indigenous and visiting, for centuries - Noel Coward, for example, wrote *Blithe Spirit* at Portmeirion and Lewis Carroll created and set *Alice in Wonderland* in Llandudno.

The metres and forms used in Welsh poetry are quite different from those in use in English. The *englyn* (an alliterative stanza) being the most popular in the early period, *Cynghanedd* (a metrical consonance peculiar to Welsh/a form of assonance) is an important feature of this early poetry and Dafydd ap Gwilym invented and popularised another distinctive metre in the form of the *cywydd*.

The Mabinogion

A masterpiece of medieval literature, *The Mabinogion*, is regarded by many as Wales' greatest contribution to European literature. The 11 folk tales in the series first came to general literary prominence in the mid-19th century but originated from around the 11th and 12th centuries and considered much older via the oral tradition.

Cantre'r Gwaelod

Seithenyn, a duty officer, was once said to have been drunk in charge of the watchtower one night at Aberdyfi and missed the tidal wave that sank *Cantre'r Gwaelod* (the hundred towns at the bottom). Borth near Aberystwyth is said to have been the 100th, his carelessness passed into folklore and Merionethshire apparently became teetotal for a decade.

The eisteddfodic tradition, male voice choirs, Tom, Shirl and the other usual suspects have long perpetuated Wales as *The Land of Song* (*Gwlad y Gân*) where the lyrical din is not confined to the 9-5. Perhaps outside loos stayed outside long enough to establish singing as the only way of getting any solitude.

The National Anthem

The Welsh national anthem is one of the oldest anthems in the world. *Hen Wlad fy Nhadau* (Land of My Fathers) was written by father and son Evan James (lyrics) and James James (tune) in 1856 and a monument to their familial accomplishment is located within Ynysangharad Park in Pontypridd.

Hen Wlad fy Nhadau (first verse and chorus)

mae hen wlad fy nhadau yn annwyl i mi

gwlad beirdd a chantorion, enwogion o fri

ei gwrol ryfelwyr gwladgarwyr tra mad

dros ryddid collasant eu gwaed

   cytgan:

gwlad! gwlad! pleidiol wyf i'm gwlad

tra môr yn fur

i'r bur hoff bau

o bydded i'r heniaith barhau

Cool Cymru

Tradition aside, the 20th century music scene promoted Wales far more than any advertising campaign. The Welsh response to *Britpop's Cool Britannia* of the mid-1990s devolved into *Cool Cymru* (*Cool Wales*) putting the country on the world map of contemporary and popular culture.

Under Milk Wood and *Moby Dick* were shot in Fishguard harbour.

Lawrence of Arabia was filmed in Merthyr Mawr sand dunes near Bridgend.

Meg Ryan starred in *Restoration* - the period backdrop being offered by Caerphilly Castle.

Snowdonia was used to film *From Russia with Love* and *First Knight* (more than 30 years apart).

The true story of *The Englishman Who Went Up a Hill But Came Down a Mountain* was built around Llanrhaeadr-ym-Mochnant.

Only Two Can Play (the first X-rated film set in Wales) was filmed in Swansea, Llanelli, Neath and Briton Ferry.

Rebecca's Daughters holds the record for the longest hiatus between the screenplay (1948) and the film's release - 44 years.

Wales has a history of developing world-class sports men and women, being passionate about rugby and building universally recognised sporting arenas.

It is the first country to birth a left-handed snooker champion, Mark Williams won the World Professional Championship in 2000.

Lawn Tennis

The 19th century adaption of an old Welsh game became known as Lawn Tennis thanks to Major Walter Wingfield from north Wales. The lawns of his home plus the publication of the rules encouraged him to patent the game. A rubber ball covered with flannel increased the game's popularity, while its simple rules made it accessible to all.

The Seven Wonders of Wales as outlined by an 18th century anonymous ink slinger:

Pistyll Rhaeadr and Wrexham steeple,

Snowdon's mountain without its people,

Overton yew trees, St Winefride's well,

Llangollen Bridge and Gresford bells.

The Stonehenge stones are originally from Pembrokeshire. They were shipped from the Preseli mountains to Wiltshire to recreate the ritual power of the region.

The world's largest camera obscura sits on top of Aberystwyth's Constitution Hill and once needed adjusting to preserve the privacy of the locals.

Pistyll Rhaeadr waterfall, with a 240 ft drop, is taller than Niagara Falls and one of the Seven Wonders of Wales. It can be found in Llanrhaeadr-ym-Mochnant, Powys, and was the 1000th Site of Special Scientific Interest (SSSI) to be notified in Wales.

Wales has more castles per square mile than any other country in Europe.

Caerphilly Castle, which stands in a 30 acre site, is the largest castle in Wales and the second largest in Europe (behind Windsor).

Trecco Bay Holiday Park at Porthcawl is Europe's largest caravan resort. It houses 1,500+ owner-occupied caravan holiday homes and almost 300 vans for hire. Trecco Bay itself is a designated *European Blue Flag* beach.

Offa's Dyke

Offa's Dyke (*Clawdd Offa*) reaches from Prestatyn to Chepstow. It is no Iron Curtain but a demarcation of the boundary between England and the 8th century newly independent Wales. It now mostly exists as a psychological barrier but you can walk along parts of it.

Millennium Stadium

Built on the site of *Cardiff Arms Park* the 40,000 sq m arena is the world's largest stadium with a retractable roof. It seats 74,500 and is almost visible from the moon.

Valleywood

Dragon International Studios Limited (dubbed 'Valleywood') is a £300 million development at Llanilid in south Wales currently under constrction. The film and TV component of the complex (occupying an area of 160 acres) will be bigger than Pinewood and Shepperton Studios combined.

Llanfairpwllgwyngyllgogerychwyrndrobwllllantysiliogogogoch

The station of Llanfair PG (the usual abbreviation) was Anglesey's first and opened in 1848. A Menai Bridge tailor is credited with the modification of the name in the 1880s and it was, for many years, the longest station name in the UK. It remains the longest official place-name in the UK and 3rd in the world.

It literally translates as:

The Church of St Mary - in the hollow of the white hazel - near the fierce whirlpool - and the Church of St Tysilio - by the red cave.

Welsh Millennium Centre

The "unmistakably Welsh and internationally outstanding" £106 million WMC has become known as Cardiff's 'armadillo'. One of the largest single private donations ever made to the arts (£20 million) helped the performing arts venue on its way to housing one of the largest theatres in Europe.

Theory of Flight

Amy Johnson took off from Pendine sands in 1933 to begin the first successful east-west transatlantic flight.

Local legend puts inventor Bill Frost in the air eight years before the Wright brothers. His 'Flying Machine' carried him above Saundersfoot in 1895...and into a tree.

Theory of Fright

In the mid to late '70s there were several sightings of UFOs in Pembrokeshire. Strange shaped aircraft and light formations were documented within the 'Dyfed Triangle'. The official line was that these 'sightings' were of the night flights from nearby RAF Aberporth, while others concluded that some LSD had been left over from the '60s.

The Daleks

Terry Nation from Cardiff conceived *The Daleks* as he was the original creator of and scriptwriter for *Doctor Who*. He apparently modelled them on the Nazis.

Mail Order Shopping

Pryce Pryce-Jones from Newtown was a 19th century draper who took advantage of the emerging railways and the reform of the postal system to develop his rural business. He would use leaflets to advertise his goods and had Florence Nightingale and Queen Victoria as customers.

Fuel Cell

Swansea man William Grove invented a fuel cell which is used by NASA to power onboard communication systems on its Apollo and Shuttle programmes.

Telegraph Printer and Microphone

A telegraph printer (the Hughes Printer - patented in 1855) was the work of David Edward Hughes from Bala along with a carbon microphone, the prototype of all microphones in use today.

Equals Sign

Robert Recorde from Tenby invented the equals sign (=) because he was 'tired of' writing equals out longhand.

He was also the first person to write mathematical textbooks in English, introducing Algebra to English speakers [yeah - thanks for that].

Telescope/Camera

The first detailed pictures of the Andromeda nebula, more than two million light years from earth, via a telescope/camera were provided by Isaac Roberts from Groes. The 'Roberts' crater on the moon is named after him.

Packet Switching

Treorchy born Donald Davies worked with *Enigma* code-breaker Alan Turing before developing 'Packet Switching'. It allows computers to communicate with each other and remains the basis of the internet.

Ronseal's Paint & Grain

Edward Prosser from Cardiff is a former painter and decorator who developed what is now the UK's biggest selling wood care product. It is also available in more than 23 countries.

Cremation

Dr William Price from Llantrisant was a 19th century medic, druid and environmentalist. In January 1884 he burned the body of his son in a ritualistic ceremony he believed was in accordance with ancient Celtic practice. He was tried but not convicted, providing for the later legalisation of cremation.

Sound Waves and Telephones

As a child William Henry Preece from Caernarvon decided that sound waves travel the same way through air as over water. He later assisted Marconi in sending the first signals across the Atlantic in 1901 - from Cornwall to Newfoundland. He also brought the first telephones to the UK, demonstrating them to Queen Victoria.

Radar

Eddie Bowen from Gendros in Swansea was a pioneer of Radar (or RDF - radio distance finding). With it the Second World War was won and he went on to invent artificial rain in the 1950s.

Psychoanalysis

Psychiatrist Ernest Jones from Gowerton has brought 'analysis', 'shrink' and 'rationalisation' into modern parlance. He organised the world's first psychiatric conference at Salzburg in conjunction with Carl Gustav Jung and became Sigmund Freud's official biographer (learning German to do it).

Natural Selection

Alfred Russel Wallace from Usk developed the theory of *Natural Selection* or 'survival of the fittest' at the same time as Charles Darwin. Extracts from the work of both were presented in a paper to the Linnean Society in 1858 and in the race to the line Darwin's *On the Origin of Species* accepted the credit.

X-rays

There is evidence to suggest that Bridgend born mathematician William Morgan produced x-rays, whilst conducting experiments on electrical discharges, more than a century before Roentgen discovered them.

David Davies - Llandinam

A major player in the construction of the Newtown to Aberystwyth railway, he later developed mines in the Rhondda. Success found 'Davies the Ocean' of The Ocean Coal Company taking on the Bute family cartel, who controlled Cardiff docks, and deciding to build his own docks at Barry instead.

John Frost - Newport, Gwent

A tailor who became a prominent member of the Chartists, campaigning for basic democratic rights. Sacked as a magistrate in 1839, he soon found himself leading 3,000 men during the *Newport Rising*. Escaping the death penalty by being transported to Australia; he returned to the UK to see most of the Chartist reforms enshrined in law.

Elizabeth Phillips Hughes - Carmarthenshire

Founded the UK's first teacher training college for women which, by 1984, had become Hughes Hall - a fully recognised college of Cambridge University. 'Bessie' Hughes was the first woman ever to achieve first class honours at degree level and campaigned for universal secondary education.

William Jones - Anglesey

In 1706 William Jones became the first person to use the Greek letter Pi (π) as a mathematical symbol to calculate the ratio of circumference to diameter of circles.

Robert Owen - Newtown

The UK's first Socialist was a mill owner who changed working conditions for his employees during the Industrial Revolution; laying the foundations for the co-operative movement and the concept of trade unions with his efforts to rid abuse of child labour and introduce profit-sharing.

Ann Pettit - Cardiff

Initiated the march from Cardiff to Greenham Common in 1981 which later grew into the Greenham Common Peace Camp. "All we asked for was a debate with our government about the siting of USA Cruise nuclear missiles in our country. This was refused so we stayed."

Spin City

Wales is home to the oldest record shop in the world. Established in 1894, the claim is made by *Spillers Records* on The Hayes in Cardiff.

Smallest House

The smallest house in the UK is at Quayside in Conwy. It is a one up one down and, according to Guinness World Records, it measures 182 x 309 x 254 cm (thats around 6 x10 x 8 ft). Its last resident, Robert Jones, was unable to stand up straight while at home and had to pee outside.

Kellogg's

Itinerant Welsh harpist Nancy Richards was visiting Dr John Harvey Kellogg when he was moving away from selling *Corn Flakes* in sacks to the boxes we see today. Seeking a brand identity he asked her for ideas, she put *ceiliog* (Welsh for cockerel) with *Kellogg* and you know the rest.

Welsh Gold

Celtic nobility wore Welsh gold as a mark of their status and the current Royal family imitates this tradition by wearing wedding rings made with the world's most valuable precious metal.

New York Mining Disaster

The *Bee Gees'* first single was inspired by the 1966 Aberfan disaster in south Wales which suffered upon the village the loss of almost an entire generation when a slag heap from the local pit crushed the school and nearby houses killing 144 people (116 were children).

'The Voice'...on the end of the line

Tom Jones received the news of his son's birth via the red phone box at the end of his road in Pontypridd. When the GPO later sold off its stock he bought the box and installed it by the pool at his Bel Air mansion. He received the news of his grandson's birth on the same phone.

Get off my Land

The last attempted invasion of mainland Britain occurred at Fishguard in 1797. It was the French who tried it on, but they were beaten back by local Jemima Nicholas with a pitchfork. The event is commemorated in the *Fishguard Tapestry*.

Prince of Wales Collar

Inspired by King Edward VIII when he was Prince of Wales the collar has become an English (sic) classic. T M Lewin shirtmakers.

Ball Boy

Neil Jenkins' junior school headmistress was once so vexed with disciplining him for fighting in the playground that she screeched at him one day "Neil Jenkins! If you want to kick anything go kick a ball." So he went on to become Wales' most capped rugby player and the world record holder for points scored in internationals (1,049).

Most Valentines Cards Sent to a Guinea Pig

On 14th February, 2001 Sooty the guinea pig received 206 cards. He broke out of his pen at Little Friends Farm the previous year, and mated with all 24 females. Guinness World Records described the rodent as "shattered" afterwards.

Death Be Not Proud

In 1956 the Death Penalty was abolished thanks to Welshman Timothy Evans. He had been wrongly convicted of murder and later became the subject of an influential book arguing against the Death Penalty. The ruling came too late for Ruth Ellis from Rhyl who, in 1955, became the last woman to be hanged in the UK.

Pirate of Non-Penance

The 'Jolly Roger' (skull and crossbones) pirates' flag is attributed to *Bartu Ddu* or *Black Bart* (he had black hair) from Pembrokeshire. As he wore a red coat the French called him 'Le Joli Rouge', which became corrupted to *Jolly Roger* and eventually synonymous with the flag.

Mount Everest

Mount Everest is named after Welshman Sir George Everest, from Crickhowell, who was Surveyor-General of India in 1865.

Don't Rain on My Parade

It doesn't rain any more in Wales than it does in England. Wales is cloudier than England though because of the hilly nature of the terrain and its proximity to the Atlantic.